W9-BXN-279

EARTH
The Incredible Recycling Machine

Paul Bennett

Thomson Learning

New York

Opposite: A view of Earth from space;
Africa can be seen clearly.

Back cover: A cheetah eating its kill,
a Thompson's gazelle.

First published in the
United States by
Thomson Learning
115 Fifth Avenue
New York, NY 10003

First published in 1993 by
Wayland (Publishers) Ltd.

Library of Congress Cataloging-in-Publication Data applied for

ISBN 1-56847-072-X

Printed in Italy

Contents

❶ The elements of life

In ancient times it was thought that everything could be broken down into four elements: earth, air, fire, and water. These broad categories seemed to account for the makeup of things until about three hundred years ago when scientists began to doubt such a simple theory.

Elements are the basic substances from which all things are made. Today we know of 109 elements. About ninety of these occur naturally on the earth – the rest are made in nuclear reactors.

Some of the elements, such as gold and silver, are metals. They have been made into jewelry since early times. The element iron, too, is a metal, and has been used to make weapons and tools for over three thousand years.

We have many elements in our bodies – about 25 of them. Oxygen and hydrogen account for most, since these elements join together to form water, and our bodies are made up of 60 to 80 percent water.

Elements are the building blocks that, in different amounts, make up all the animals, plants, rocks, water, and air.

Water is a compound – a combination of elements. So is the paper on which these words are printed. Paper is made of a material called cellulose, which comes from trees and consists of the elements carbon, hydrogen, and oxygen.

Harvesting onions. The farmer will need to replace the vital elements that are removed from the soil with each crop.

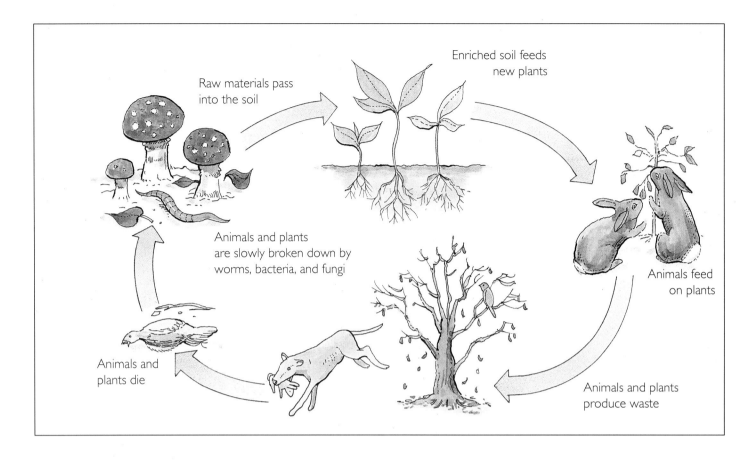

Raw materials pass
into the soil

Enriched soil feeds
new plants

Animals and plants
are slowly broken down by
worms, bacteria, and fungi

Animals feed
on plants

Animals and
plants die

Animals and plants
produce waste

Elements and compounds are needed by all living things in order to stay alive. Living organisms obtain these raw materials or resources from their surroundings. But only limited amounts of these vital elements can be found on Earth, and so if they could be used only once, they would run out, and animals and plants would die. But in nature the elements are recycled, so they can be used over and over again.

For example, when animals and plants die in a woodland, they are slowly broken down by worms, bacteria, and fungi. As animals and

ABOVE **In nature, the process of death, decay, new life, and growth ensures that vital resources are recycled.**

plants rot away, the substances from which they are made pass into the soil. The enriched soil feeds new plants and, in turn, animals will feed on the plants. The animals and plants produce waste, which is also broken down and taken back into the soil.

The process of death, decay, new life, and growth is never ending. In this way, the elements and compounds that are essential to life are recycled.

ABOVE **A forest in British Columbia, Canada. The resources that helped this rotting tree to grow will pass into the soil and feed new plants.**

However, the activities of people have upset this delicate natural balance. Vital resources such as water and the elements carbon, nitrogen, sulfur, and phosphorus are no longer in balance. As a result, a large number of animal and plant species are in danger.

By understanding the earth's recycling systems and how people affect them, we can help reduce the harmful effects of human activity.

❷ The water cycle

ABOVE **A Brazilian boy bringing fresh water in cans from the village well. To keep healthy, people must drink clean water regularly.**

Although our planet is called Earth, almost three-quarters of it is covered by water. Ninety percent of this water is found in the seas and oceans. It is not surprising, then, that water – a combination of the chemical elements hydrogen and oxygen – is the commonest compound on Earth.

Water is very useful since it is able to dissolve or melt many substances, including the nutrients that plants need in order to grow. Once dissolved, the nutrients become thoroughly mixed with the groundwater, which plants take in through their roots.

Water not only dissolves and transports nutrients through the soil, it moves them through the bodies of plants and animals as well. Blood is made up mostly of water, and this circulates nutrients throughout our bodies through blood vessels called arteries and veins. Water is also essential to the body because it carries away waste.

RIGHT **The nutrients dissolved in groundwater are taken into plants through the roots.**

Without plants, animals (including people) could not exist. All our food comes originally from food made by plants. We eat the plants themselves – potatoes, peas, and rice, for example. And the meat that we eat comes from plant-eating animals such as cows and sheep. The way food energy from plants passes into plant-eating animals and on into meat-eating animals is called the food chain.

Water can absorb harmful chemicals, too. If these chemicals are taken in by plants, they can affect their growth or even cause them to die. And because animals, including people, eat plants, they can be affected as well.

Water is very special because it occurs naturally in several forms: as the liquid that falls to earth as rain; as a gas in the form of water vapor, which is in the air we breathe; and as a solid when frozen into ice.

Most of the water that falls as rain comes from the sea. The sun heats the sea, causing tiny particles of water to drift up from the surface into the air. This process is known as evaporation. Water also evaporates from lakes and rivers, and from the leaves of trees and plants. When the air cools, the moisture in the air condenses (changes from water vapor into water droplets), and clouds form. Eventually, water droplets in the clouds become large and heavy enough to fall as rain.

Some of this rainwater enters the soil, where it may be soaked up by underground rocks, or it may seep into rivers or lakes. The rest of the water runs along the surface of the land and returns to the sea in streams and rivers, where the whole process of evaporation begins again. This is called the water cycle.

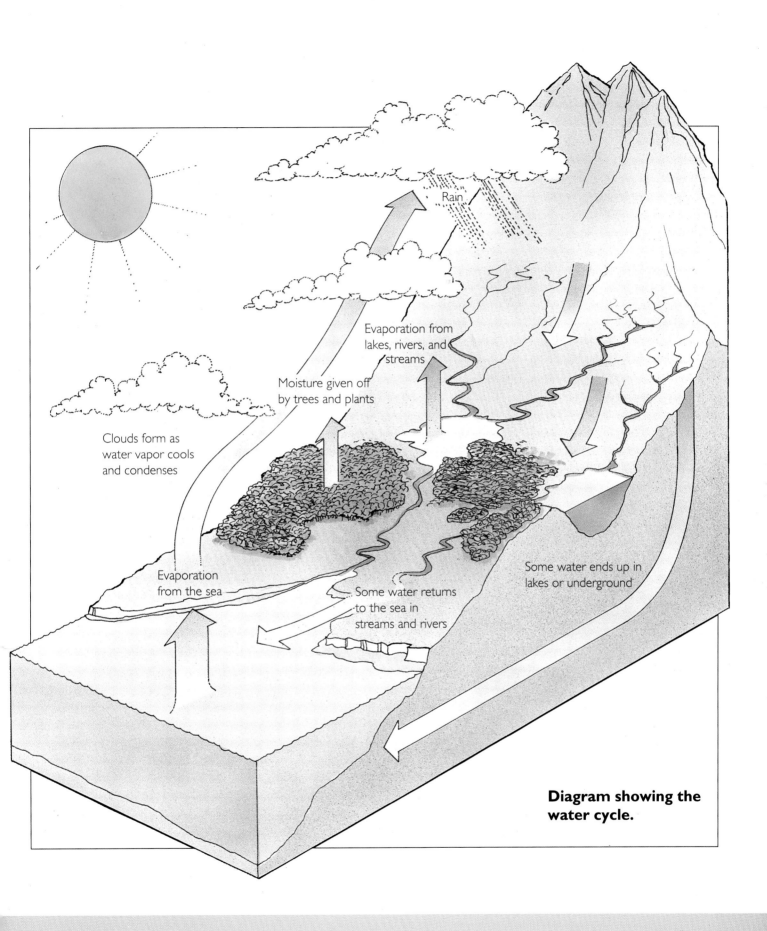

Rain

Evaporation from
lakes, rivers, and
streams

Moisture given off
by trees and plants

Clouds form as
water vapor cools
and condenses

Evaporation
from the sea

Some water returns
to the sea in
streams and rivers

Some water ends up in
lakes or underground

**Diagram showing the
water cycle.**

When water vapor rises into the sky at the start of the water cycle, impurities are left behind. The rain that falls from the clouds should then be clean. But is it? No – the chemicals in the smoke from our factories, power plants, and cars are absorbed by the moisture in the air.

This dirty water at Zeebrugge, Belgium, is polluted by chemicals and untreated sewage.

So, as the rain falls it is polluted. In the chapter on the sulfur cycle (page 28), you can learn how acid rain is produced and the effects it can have on our environment.

The chemical pesticides sprayed on crops can be washed by the rain into rivers.

We are able to interrupt the flow of the water cycle. The water that comes from our faucets originally fell to the earth as rain. But it does not rain every day, and so we trap some of the rainwater in artificial lakes called reservoirs. The water from reservoirs passes through pipes to cleaning and pumping stations, and then is piped to our homes and factories.

Untreated wastewater, or sewage, from homes and factories contains harmful bacteria and chemicals. If a small amount of the waste gets into rivers and lakes, other bacteria can eat up much of it, while the rest sinks harmlessly to the bottom. But a large amount of sewage will overload the natural process and cause pollution. That is why much of the sewage is cleaned at a treatment plant before it is pumped back into rivers. However, even this "clean" sewage contains chemicals, such as phosphates, that damage life in streams and rivers.

These people in the Amazon region of South America do not have homes with running water. They wash their clothes and bathe in the nearest stream, which may be polluted.

Untreated sewage is often pumped out to sea, but it is sometimes washed back onto the beaches, where it causes pollution. In many countries, the only source of water is a polluted river or pond. In these countries, everyday activities, such as washing clothes and bathing, may cause people to catch diseases.

Farmers use chemicals to fertilize the soil and kill pests that attack their crops. These chemicals can be washed by rain into the groundwater that drains into rivers, which will then be polluted. In some areas where water is scarce, underground water is pumped to the surface for people to use. Sometimes this water may also be polluted by the chemicals used in farming.

❸ The nitrogen cycle

The element nitrogen is a gas that cannot be seen or smelled, yet it makes up 78 percent of the air we breathe. (The other main gas in the atmosphere is the element oxygen, which makes up 21 percent of our air.)

Nitrogen is essential for life since it is part of DNA, which is the "blueprint" of every cell in all living things. DNA controls the way characteristics, or features, are passed on from one generation to the next. One of these characteristics is eye color. If you have pets such as rabbits, cats, or hamsters, you may see similarities between the different generations. The similarities are carried from parents to their young through DNA.

Nitrogen is one of the ingredients of proteins, which are essential for healthy growth. Proteins form the substance of which muscles, skin, and organs are made. Plants also need proteins, which build strong stems and healthy leaves.

RIGHT **Nitrogen is an ingredient of proteins, which we need for healthy growth.**

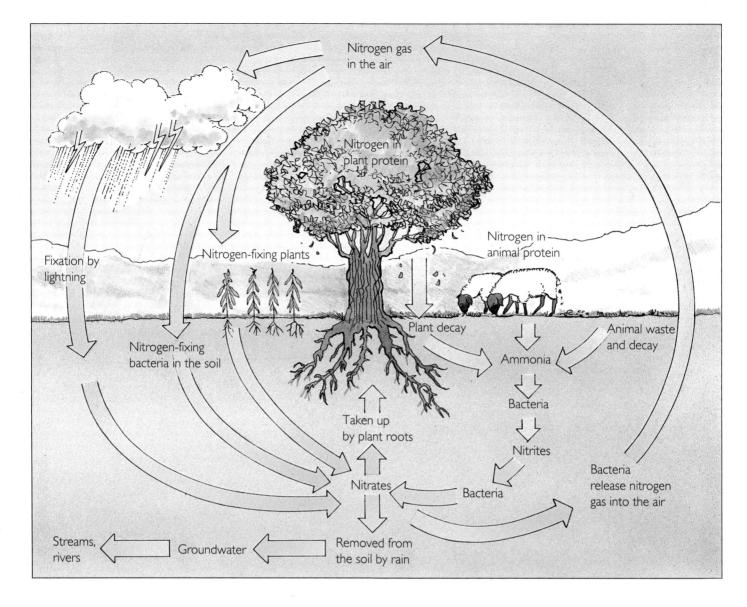

Labels within diagram:
- Nitrogen gas in the air
- Nitrogen in plant protein
- Nitrogen in animal protein
- Fixation by lightning
- Nitrogen-fixing plants
- Nitrogen-fixing bacteria in the soil
- Plant decay
- Animal waste and decay
- Ammonia
- Bacteria
- Nitrites
- Bacteria release nitrogen gas into the air
- Taken up by plant roots
- Nitrates
- Bacteria
- Streams, rivers
- Groundwater
- Removed from the soil by rain

Although nitrogen is in the air in vast amounts, for most forms of life, nitrogen in the form of gas is useless. Animals obtain their nitrogen by feeding on plants or other animals. Plants use nitrogen that has been "fixed" in the soil. This means nitrogen has been taken from the air and changed so that plants can absorb it and use it for growth.

Diagram showing the nitrogen cycle in nature.

Since Roman times, it has been known that some plants, such as beans and clover, can enrich poor overused soil. Today we know that this is because there are millions of bacteria living in the knoblike roots of these plants. The bacteria are able

RIGHT **The knoblike roots of a nitrogen-fixing plant.**

to take nitrogen in the air and "fix" it as chemicals called nitrates. The nitrates dissolve in water and are taken into plants through the roots. The plants can then use the nitrogen in the nitrates to make protein, which is needed for healthy growth.

Nitrogen can also become fixed in the soil during thunderstorms. The lightning joins together some of the oxygen and nitrogen in the air to form compounds called nitrogen oxides. These react with the rain-water to produce weak acids that fall

A storm over Tucson, Arizona. Nitrogen can become fixed in the soil during thunderstorms.

on the soil and then become nitrates.

When animals and plants die and decay, the nitrogen in their proteins is released into the soil in the form of a chemical called ammonia. Waste from living animals also contains nitrogen in the form of ammonia. Some bacteria in the soil break down

the ammonia into nitrogen gas, which escapes into the atmosphere. Other bacteria break down the ammonia into a substance that is changed into nitrates. These nitrates can then be taken up by plants.

Nitrogen is quickly removed from the soil by plants, and it may also be easily washed out of the soil by

18

rainwater. Because of this, farmers regularly put chemical fertilizers on the land to boost the level of nitrates for the plants to absorb. This makes the plants stronger and also allows more of them to grow.

The benefit to farmers of putting nitrogen on the soil is that they can produce enough food to feed the world's growing population. But because nitrates can be easily carried through the soil, they find their way into groundwater and rivers. These may be used as sources of drinking water. In areas with a large number of farms, the amount of nitrates found in drinking water is often above safe limits.

A muckspreader being loaded. Farmyard muck is a natural fertilizer that is rotted before it is spread on the land to improve the soil.

For hundreds of years farmers have used natural fertilizers from farmyard animals to improve the quality of the soil. These natural fertilizers release their nutrients slowly and produce less pollution than chemical fertilizers.

Chemical fertilizers release their nutrients quickly, and this allows plants to grow faster. However, a rainstorm can wash the fertilizer's nutrients out of the soil before they get used.

Farmers used to change the crop grown in a particular field every year. They might grow wheat in a field one year, followed the next year by peas or another nitrogen-fixing crop. Sometimes a field was left fallow – no crops were planted at all – and weeds, clover, and grass were allowed to grow. These plants were later plowed into the ground where they would rot and fertilize the soil. In order to produce more food, farmers in many parts of the world have not kept up the system of crop rotation.

Even human feces can be used as a natural fertilizer if it is treated first. When it is treated at the sewage plant, the water is made clean and the solids (sludge) are left. These solids are often disposed of at sea or in landfill sites, or they are burned.

This is wasteful because the sludge contains nutrients that plants need in order to grow. Sludge can also help to improve the soil, making it better for plant growth. However, sludge sometimes contains poisonous chemicals and metals, such as lead and mercury. These come from wastewater from factories that is piped to the sewage plant. These poisons must be removed from the sludge before it is put on the land.

BELOW **Rice being harvested in California. To produce large crops year after year, farmers have to add enormous quantities of fertilizers to the fields.**

4 The phosphorus cycle

The name phosphorus comes from a Greek word that means "bringer of light." This is because the element white phosphorus glows in the dark and catches fire when it comes into contact with the air.

Phosphorus is essential to all forms of life, first of all because it is part of DNA – the "code" that controls characteristics passed from parent to child. Phosphorus is also found in a compound called ATP, which stores energy needed by cells – for the action of muscles, for example. And phosphorus is also needed for healthy bones. Children who do not get enough of it suffer from a disease of the bones called rickets. Their bones are "softer" than normal and bend out of shape. In adults, a

RIGHT **Phosphorus helps to make our bones strong and well shaped. It also helps our muscles work when we exercise.**

lack of phosphorus causes bones to break easily, and may sometimes lead to twitching and jumping muscles in the face, hands, and feet.

We take in about .04 ounces of phosphorus per day in the form of chemicals called phosphates, and we store about 26 ounces of it in our bones in the form of calcium phosphate.

Phosphorus is one of the scarcest of the elements that are naturally recycled. It is recycled in different ways. Some is returned to the soil when plants and animals die. It is

The droppings of seabirds are called guano. Guano from the coast of Peru was once used as fertilizer. Sailors loaded the guano onto their boats and sailed back home, where the cargo was sold to farmers.

taken up by plants, which are then eaten by animals. When we eat plants or plant-eating animals, we obtain much of the phosphorus we need to stay healthy.

Much phosphorus is held in rocks and recycled when rocks are broken down by the action of the rain, wind, and ice. Because it is easily dissolved in rainwater, phosphorus is carried

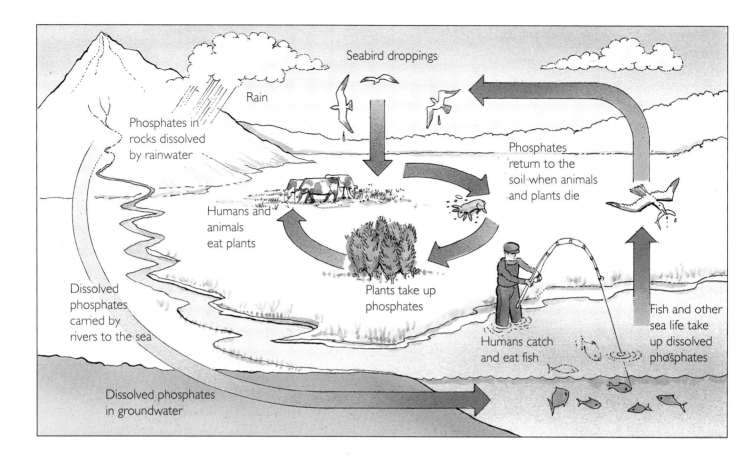

Diagram showing the phosphorus cycle.

away to rivers, which flow into the sea. Every year millions of tons of phosphorus are dissolved from rocks and carried out to sea. Fish and other sea life take up the dissolved phosphorus. By eating fish, we get some of the phosphorus we need.

Seabirds, such as gulls and pelicans, also catch and eat fish. Their droppings on the land provide a source of phosphorus for plants around our coastlines. The phosphorus helps roots to grow and buds to form on plants.

Today, however, because of the way we live, we may be releasing too much phosphorus into the environment too fast. Phosphorus mined from phosphate rock is used in fertilizer, which is added to the soil to help up grow large crops. And phosphorus is used in other ways. For example, we use it to improve the cleaning power of detergents.

All this phosphorus can cause problems. Phosphorus dissolves easily in water. The water from our washing machines, the runoff from farms, and the waste from our toilets all can pollute our rivers and lakes.

In most areas, waste matter or sewage is carried by sewers to a treatment plant. There the solids and liquids are separated, and the liquids are "cleaned" and returned to the river. However, these "clean" liquids can still contain phosphates.

A phosphate refinery in the North African country of Tunisia. Phosphate rock is mined in many places around the world.

The phosphates from farms and sewage treatment plants can build up in slow-moving water, such as ponds

A Canadian sewage farm. The "clean" water that is returned to the river can still contain phosphates.

or lakes. The phosphates, together with nitrates mainly from farms, are used as food by simple plants called algae. As a result, a green slimy mass of algae quickly forms on the water and eventually keeps the sunlight from reaching the plants deeper down. Without sunlight, the plants cannot produce oxygen. With less oxygen in the water, fish cannot breathe. And when the algae die, bacteria feed on them, using up the remaining oxygen in the water. Water snails and insect larvae also die. Soon the pond or lake becomes lifeless.

In nature's recycling, much of the phosphorus is dissolved slowly from rock and flows into rivers. It does not have a chance to build up. And algae cannot grow rapidly out of control in fast-flowing water. It is the phosphorus that is artificially added to our environment that can cause harm.

RIGHT **Unpolluted ponds are full of life. Here a water beetle feeds on a stickleback.**

LEFT **Algae growing on the surface of a pond. Ponds covered by algae soon become lifeless.**

5 **The sulfur cycle**

Sulfur is another important element. It is a yellow substance that is found in the ground and burns easily. Sulfur was known to ancient civilizations – in the Bible, it is referred to as brimstone. About two thousand years ago sulfur was used by the Chinese to make gunpowder for fireworks. It is still used to make gunpowder and matches. Sulfur is also used to make sulfuric acid, which is a very important industrial chemical used in fertilizers, dyes, and explosives.

Kilauea, a volcano in Hawaii, sending a shower of molten lava into the air. Sulfur is found in volcanic rocks.

Sulfur is found all over the world, especially in volcanic rocks. It is also found in sedimentary rocks, which were formed from deposits laid down by water, ice, or wind. In the United States, sedimentary rocks containing sulfur are especially common along the coasts of Texas and Louisiana. Sulfur is also found in coal, natural gas, and many other different substances that can be found in the ground.

Sulfur is essential to all living things. It occurs in proteins, which are vital to our bodies; they form the material from which muscles, tissues, and organs are made. On average, people have five ounces of sulfur in their bodies, and everyone takes in a tiny bit of sulfur every day.

In nature, sulfur is recycled every time plants and animals die. As they decay, substances called sulfates, which can easily combine with water, are taken up or absorbed by the roots of growing plants.

Animals get the sulfur they need to stay healthy by eating plants or, if they are hunters, by eating prey that are plant-eaters. In places such as swamps where the soil is waterlogged, there is a type of bacteria that can turn sulfates into a gas that smells of rotten eggs.

RIGHT **A tiger with a sambur cow it has just killed. Animal hunters get the sulfur they need by eating plant-eaters.**

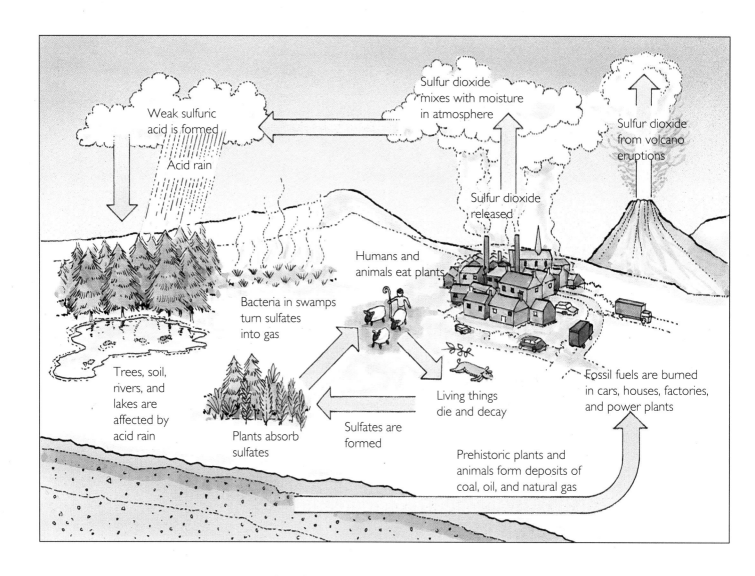

Labels in the diagram:

Weak sulfuric acid is formed

Acid rain

Sulfur dioxide mixes with moisture in atmosphere

Sulfur dioxide from volcano eruptions

Sulfur dioxide released

Humans and animals eat plants

Bacteria in swamps turn sulfates into gas

Trees, soil, rivers, and lakes are affected by acid rain

Plants absorb sulfates

Sulfates are formed

Living things die and decay

Fossil fuels are burned in cars, houses, factories, and power plants

Prehistoric plants and animals form deposits of coal, oil, and natural gas

Diagram showing the sulfur cycle.

If the balance of the sulfur cycle is upset, animals and plants will suffer. One way this has happened is through the burning of coal, oil, and gas. These fossil fuels were formed millions of years ago from dead rain-forest plants or from the bodies of tiny creatures called plankton. We burn fossil fuels to make energy for use in power plants, factories, and vehicles. As they burn, the sulfur in them is released as a gas called sulfur

ABOVE **Sulfur dioxide from factories pollutes the air.**

dioxide, which goes up into the atmosphere. Sulfur dioxide pollutes the air, and when moisture in the atmosphere mixes with the gas, weak sulfuric acid is formed. This can be carried in the air for hundreds of miles by the wind. When it falls to the ground, it is called acid rain or acid snow.

Acid rain is not new – sulfur dioxide from swamps and volcanic eruptions has always been in the air. But until now the environment has been able to adjust to its effects. The difference today is that the rain is much more polluted with acids from other sources, such as the burning of fossil fuels for energy.

The trees in this Polish national park have been killed by acid rain.

Because the clouds can be blown by the winds for hundreds of miles, polluted rain can cause harm a long way from the original source of the pollution. In Europe, one of the worst-affected areas is Scandinavia. The pollution is carried there from Britain, Germany, and eastern European countries. In North America, Canada claims that much of its acid rain is caused by pollution from the United States.

RIGHT **Acid rain has damaged this stone sculpture in Kraków, Poland.**

Acid rain is most serious in or near big industrial areas. It can directly attack the leaves and needles of trees, and it can soak into the soil and damage plants and trees through their roots. Some forests in eastern Europe have been destroyed by acid rain. Many lakes in Scandinavia, Scotland, and Canada are without fish. The acid rain releases poisons into the water, so lake animals and plants are killed, too.

Acid rain eats into stone and concrete, slowly destroying buildings. It also makes metal rust more quickly, so steel bridges have to be painted constantly to prevent the acid from eating away at the bare metal.

❻ The carbon cycle

BELOW **Millions of years ago, huge swampy forests like this covered much of the earth. The ground was thick with rotting trees and plants which, over long periods of time, became coal.**

Carbon is a very common element, and it is found in a number of forms, such as coal, coke, carbon black, graphite, and diamond. A diamond is the hardest substance known, and because of its beauty, it is a precious stone. Graphite, on the other hand, is soft and, when mixed with clay, is used as the "lead" in

pencils. Coal and coke are burned to provide heat, and carbon black is used in the making of inks, carbon paper, typewriter ribbons, and paint.

Carbon is the basis of all life, since it is part of DNA. The adult human body contains about 35 pounds of carbon in one form or another. It combines with such elements as hydrogen, oxygen, and nitrogen to form about 18 percent of all the matter in our bodies.

A coal-fired power plant. Coal, gas, and oil are called fossil fuels and are burned to provide heat and power.

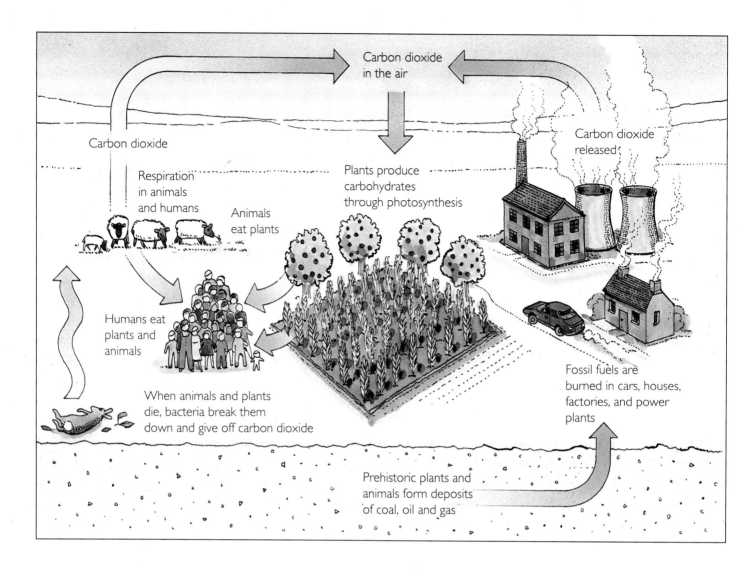

Labels within the diagram:

Carbon dioxide in the air

Carbon dioxide

Carbon dioxide released

Respiration in animals and humans

Animals eat plants

Plants produce carbohydrates through photosynthesis

Humans eat plants and animals

When animals and plants die, bacteria break them down and give off carbon dioxide

Fossil fuels are burned in cars, houses, factories, and power plants

Prehistoric plants and animals form deposits of coal, oil and gas

Carbon circulates through the environment in many different forms, and it combines with other elements to become compounds. In living things carbon exists as the gas carbon dioxide. There is only a very small amount of carbon dioxide in the air, but without it, plants would not be able to make their own food and grow. The process by which green plants make their own food substances is called photosynthesis.

Diagram showing the carbon cycle. All living things contain carbon.

In the process of photosynthesis, carbon dioxide in the air is absorbed through tiny pores in a plant's leaves. With light energy from the sun, the carbon dioxide is combined with water from the plant's roots. When this happens, oxygen is made, along with carbohydrates, which are the plant's food.

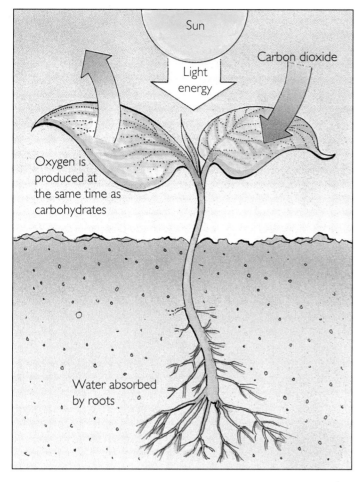

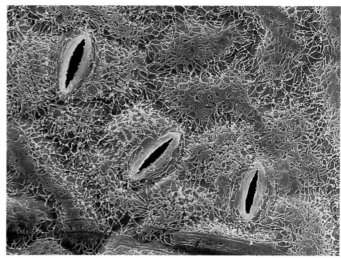

LEFT **This diagram shows the process of photosynthesis in green plants.**

ABOVE **A highly magnified picture of a leaf showing its tiny pores.**

The energy that animals (including humans) get from carbohydrates is released only after complicated reactions involving oxygen, which is breathed in. As the energy is released, we breathe out carbon dioxide and water. These are waste products from our bodies. The whole process is known as respiration.

Plants give oxygen to us, and in return we give carbon dioxide to them. Plants and animals are dependent on each other. But what happens if this delicate cycle is upset?

The level of carbon dioxide in the atmosphere is increasing. About twenty billion tons of carbon dioxide are put into the atmosphere every year from burning fossil fuels. As we have seen, coal, gas, and oil are the remains of plants and animals that died millions of years ago. When they burn, the carbon that is contained in them is released in the form of carbon dioxide. Plants are unable to absorb this extra carbon dioxide.

When rain-forest trees are burned, carbon dioxide is released into the air, adding to the greenhouse effect.

Although most of the extra carbon dioxide is caused by the burning of fossil fuels, some of the increase is due to the destruction of vast areas of rain forest. At present, an area the size of Georgia is being destroyed every year. Unless the destruction stops, there will be no rain forest left within forty years. The loss of huge numbers of trees means that less of the carbon dioxide people produce is being absorbed through photosynthesis. Trees also contain carbon, and when the trees are burned the carbon is released as carbon dioxide.

RIGHT **Flooded fields in California. The greenhouse effect could result in a rise in sea level, flooding many of the world's major cities and much good farmland.**

Most scientists believe that the buildup of carbon dioxide is the main cause of global warming. The gas acts like the panes of glass in a greenhouse. It allows the heat of the sun to reach the earth, but traps some of the heat that would normally escape back into space. As a result, the atmosphere is getting warmer. The result is known as the greenhouse effect.

It is generally accepted that in the next fifty years, the temperature of our planet will increase by 2.7°F.

This seemingly small increase in temperature could, in fact, start the melting of the ice caps of the North and South Poles. A rise of only three feet could flood vast areas of low-lying land and islands across the world.

The greenhouse effect may also change the world's weather patterns, causing droughts in some areas and torrential rain in others. This could mean that an important crop-growing area today could become too dry or wet to grow food in the future.

❼ Living in tune with the cycles

In this book you have read about nature's delicate cycles, which can be upset very easily. Each one of us can help to keep these cycles in balance by being thoughtful about what we do and the things we buy. For example, there are laundry detergents that do not contain phosphates which, as you have read, can lead to polluted and lifeless ponds and lakes. We can also buy vegetables and cereals that have been produced organically. This means that only

We can all help the environment by using phosphate-free laundry detergent.

Scrubbing vegetables using a bowl of water instead of under a running tap saves water.

natural fertilizers have been used on the land to produce them. Although organically-grown food costs more, organic farming is better for the natural cycles than farming that uses chemicals on the land or the crops.

The way we prepare food can also help the natural cycles. Washing fruit and vegetables under a running faucet wastes water. By using a bowl, less water is used and the wastewater can go onto the garden instead of down the drain. Vegetable peelings can be put on a compost heap, so that the nutrients in the peelings can be returned to the soil.

LEFT **Packaging is necessary, but some goods are over-packaged. You can help the environment by buying items that are not over-packaged.**

The burning of fossil fuels has led to an increase in temperatures around the world and also to the problem of acid rain. The waste gases that come from chimneys can be filtered, and cars can be made to produce less pollution. But not all countries are willing to pass laws that would remove the causes of these problems.

One way we can all reduce acid rain pollution and global warming is to use less energy. By using less energy, we can reduce the amount of fossil fuels that we burn at power plants. In the home, attics and walls can be insulated and windows can be double-glazed to prevent heat from escaping. These methods conserve fossil fuels and save us money.

We can also use buses and trains more often in order to save fuel.

Public transportation is more friendly to our environment than cars because more people can be carried for the same amount of fuel. Walking and bicycling do not pollute the environment or use up precious fuel, and they help us to stay fit and healthy.

In the future, our supplies of fossil fuels will not be enough for our needs. It is possible to use natural sources of energy that do not run out. These are called renewable sources of energy. They include wind and wave power, energy from natural heat deep in the earth's crust, energy from the sun, and hydroelectric power (using the power of falling water to make electricity). All these energy sources cause little or no pollution, and none are harmful to the earth's natural cycles.

OPPOSITE **A busy street full of cars and taxis in New York. Cars and other vehicles use a lot of fuel and cause harmful pollution.**

LEFT **Sorting glass and plastics at a recycling center. The best way to dispose of waste is to recycle it.**

Recycling saves precious resources and energy. Plastics, glass, paper and cardboard, and aluminum cans can all be recycled. Find out where your local recycling center is and encourage your family and friends to recycle their household waste.

When you go shopping, choose items that are not over-packaged, and reuse your old plastic bags to carry them home in. Also, try to buy items that will not damage the environment. For example, clothes that can be washed are better than those that can only be dry-cleaned, since dry-cleaning chemicals can damage the layer of gas in the atmosphere called the ozone layer.

The ozone layer is important because it absorbs the sun's harmful ultraviolet (UV) rays. The UV rays slow down the growth of plants, which are vital to the natural cycles. They can also cause skin cancer and eye problems in humans. The ozone layer is damaged by CFCs, which are chemicals that used to be used in some spray cans and to make some kinds of packing foam.

There are many other ways in which we can all help our environment and the natural cycles. Here are some suggestions:

● Find out as much as possible about environmental issues and discuss them with your family and friends.

● Write down a list of what you think are the most serious environmental issues and the ones that you think you can do something about.

● Join an environmental organization and tell your friends about the work it does, and why the environment is so important.

Try to think for yourself about environmental issues and to do what you think is right. Your actions can make a difference to the environment that we all share.

A beach scene in New South Wales, Australia. The child in pink is wearing special clothing to protect his skin against the sun's harmful UV rays.

Glossary

Algae A group of simple plants, which includes most seaweeds.

Ammonia A strong-smelling gas made of hydrogen and nitrogen.

ATP Adenosine triphosphate. A substance found in all plant and animal cells. ATP is a major source of energy for the cell.

Bacteria Living things that have only one cell. They are found in the air, water, earth, living and dead bodies, and rotting things.

Blueprint A sketch-plan of work to be done.

Carbohydrates Substances that contain carbon, hydrogen, and oxygen.

Carbon black A form of carbon used in pigments (colors) in the making of paints, for example.

Carbon dioxide A gas present in the air and breathed out by animals, including humans.

Chemical A substance that is formed by a chemical process. Chemistry is the study of the way the elements in a substance combine and react with everything else.

Compound A substance made from two or more elements.

Decay Decompose. To break down and rot.

Detergents Liquids and powders used for washing dishes, clothes, and other things.

DNA Deoxyribonucleic acid – found in nearly all living organisms. It controls what is passed on from one generation to another.

Elements The basic substances from which all things are made.

Environment The natural world around us – plants, animals, rivers, and rocks, for example.

Environmental issues Topics and subjects having to do with the environment.

Evaporation The changing of a liquid into a gas. For example, water evaporates, or changes to water vapor, when heated.

Fertile Used to describe soil rich in nutrients that can support a large number of crops.

Fertilizer A manure or chemical that is used to enrich the soil and help plants to grow.

Fossil fuels Natural fuels, such as coal, oil, or gas. Fossil fuels were formed underground, over millions of years, from the remains of prehistoric animals and plants.

Fungi Plants such as toadstools, mushrooms, and molds that feed on the remains of dead plants and animals.

Generation A single step in family descent, such as mother to daughter.

Global warming The warming up of Earth's surface due to the buildup in the Earth's atmosphere of gases (such as carbon dioxide), which trap the sun's heat.

Insulated Covered with a material that will not allow electrical currents, heat, or sound to pass through.

Nuclear reactor A device in a nuclear power plant that is used in the production of nuclear energy.

Nutrients Substances, such as minerals and water, that plants and animals need to live and grow.

Photosynthesis The process by which nearly all plants can use sunlight to turn water and carbon dioxide into food.

Polluted Made dirty or impure.

Population All the persons living in a particular place.

Prey Animals that may be killed by others for food.

Protein A substance (present in milk, eggs, and meat, for example) that is necessary for all living things.

Recycle To use again instead of discarding.

Respiration Breathing.

Sedimentary rocks Rocks formed from sediments – material transported by ice or flowing water.

Species A group of plants or animals that are alike in most ways.

Useful addresses

Environmental Law Institute
1616 P Street NW
Suite 200
Washington, DC 20036

Friends of the Earth
218 D Street SE
Washington, DC 20003

Greenpeace USA
1436 U Street NW
Washington, DC 20009

National Parks and Conservation Association
1015 31st Street NW
Washington, DC 20007

Sierra Club
730 Polk Street
San Francisco, CA 94109

United States Committee for the
   United Nations Environment Program
2013 Q Street NW
Washington, DC 20009

World Wildlife Fund
1250 24th Street
Washington, DC 20037

Books to read

Conserving Our World – a series about global solutions to global environmental problems. Published in Austin by Raintree Steck-Vaughn.
Domestic Waste by Tony Hare. Save Our Earth. New York: Gloucester Press, 1992.
Ecology and Conservation by Steven Seidenberg. Milwaukee: Gareth Stevens, 1990.
Exploring Humans and the Environment by John Baines. Austin: Raintree Steck-Vaughn, 1992.
The Green Activity Book by Meryl Doney. Batavia, IL: Lion USA, 1991.
How Green Are You? by David Bellamy. New York: Crown Books for Young Readers, 1991.
The Plant Cycle by Nina Morgan. Natural Cycles. New York: Thomson Learning, 1993.
Protecting the Planet by Colin Harris. Young Geographer. New York: Thomson Learning, 1993.
What We Can Do About – a series showing young people how they can help to take care of the environment. Published in New York by Franklin Watts.

Picture acknowledgments

Bruce Coleman Ltd *back cover* (William S. Paton), 20 (D. Meredith), 27 top (Jane Burton), 12 and 29 (J-P Zwaenepoel); Environmental Picture Library 12 (Daphne Christelis), 38 (H. Girardet), 40 (C. MacPherson); Geoscience Features 26 (W. Pierdon); Hutchison Library 23 (Robert Francis), 25 (J. Reditt); Image Select *front cover, contents page*; Natural History Museum 34; Christine Osborne Pictures 45; Oxford Scientific Films 9 (Dr. G. I. Bernard), 17 (Breck P. Kent); Science Photo Library 13 and 21 bottom (Peter Menzel), 27 bottom and 37 (Dr. Jeremy Burgess), 32 and 33 top (Simon Fraser); Tony Stone Worldwide 18-19, 28 (Denis Oda), 31 (Keith Wood), 43 (Ken Biggs), 44 (Jon Riley); Wayland Picture Library 4, 5 (C. Osborne), 7 (Chris Fairclough), 10, 8 and 14 (Julia Waterlow), 15, 22, 35, 42; Tim Woodcock 41; Zefa 39, 43. The illustrations are by Stephen Wheele.

Index